THE 4 CHORD COUNTRY SONGBOOK

Garth Brooks • Brooks & Dunn • Mary Chapin Carpenter

Johnny Cash • Rosanne Cash • Terri Clark • Billy Ray Cyrus

John Denver • Joe Diffie • Dixie Chicks • ~~...~~ *Jackson*

Toby Keith • Hal Ketchum • Alison Kr~~...~~ *...ation*

Kris Kristofferson • Patty Loveless • Kathy Mattea

Martina McBride • Tim McGraw • Buck Owens • Dolly Parton

Charlie Pride • Kenny Rogers • SHeDAISY • George Strait

Aaron Tippin • Randy Travis • Shania Twain • Jeanne Pruett

Hank Williams • Lucinda Williams

ISBN: 978-1-4803-1258-6

Visit our website at www.cherrylaneprint.com

Contents

Achy Breaky Heart (Don't Tell My Heart)

Words and Music by
Don Von Tress

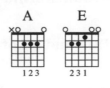

Verse 1

A
You can tell the world you never was my girl.

A   **|E**
You can burn my clothes when I'm gone.

  |E
Or you can tell your friends just what a fool I've been

  |E   **|A**
And laugh and joke about me on the phone.

A
You can tell my arms go back to the farm.

A   **|E**
You can tell my feet to hit the floor.

  |E
Or you can tell my lips to tell my fingertips

  |E   **|A**
They won't be reaching out for you no more.

Chorus

A
Don't tell my heart, my achy breaky heart.

|A   **|E**
I just don't think he'd under - stand.

  |E
And if you tell my heart, my achy breaky heart,

  |E   **|A**
He might blow up and kill this man. Ooh.

Achy Breaky Heart (Don't Tell My Heart)

Words and Music by
Don Von Tress

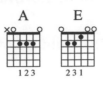

A   E

1 2 3   2 3 1

Verse 1

A | |
You can tell the world you never was my girl.

A |**E**
You can burn my clothes when I'm gone.

    |**E** |
Or you can tell your friends just what a fool I've been

      |**E** |**A** |
And laugh and joke about me on the phone.

A | |
You can tell my arms go back to the farm.

A |**E**
You can tell my feet to hit the floor.

    |**E** |
Or you can tell my lips to tell my fingertips

      |**E** |**A**   ‖
They won't be reaching out for you no more.

Chorus

A |
Don't tell my heart, my achy breaky heart.

 |**A** |**E**
I just don't think he'd under - stand.

    |**E** |
And if you tell my heart, my achy breaky heart,

    |**E** |**A**   ‖
He might blow up and kill this man. Ooh.

Verse 2

A | |
You can tell your ma I moved to Arkansas.

A |E
You can tell your dog to bite my leg.

|E |
Or tell your brother Cliff whose fist can tell my lip.

|E |A
He never really liked me any - way.

|A |
Or tell your Aunt Louise. Tell anything you please.

| |E
My - self already knows I'm not o - kay.

|E |
Or you can tell my eyes to watch out for my mind.

|E |A ||
It might be walking out on me to - day.   But

Repeat Chorus

Repeat Chorus

Act Naturally

Words and Music by
Vonie Morrison and Johnny Russell

D   G   A7   E7

Verse 1

D | **|G** | |
They're gonna put me in the movies;

D | **|A7** |
They're gonna make a big star out of me.

|D | **|G** |
We'll make a scene about a man that's sad and lonely,

|A7 | **|D** |
And all I gotta do is   act natural - ly.

Verse 2

||D | **|G** |
We'll make a score about a man that's sad and lonely

|D | **|A7** |
And beggin' down up - on his bended knee.

|D | **|G** |
I'll play the part but I won't need re - hearsin',

|A7 | **|D** |
'Cause all I have to do is   act natural - ly.

Bridge

‖**A7** | |**D** |
Well, I bet you I'm gonna be a big star.

|**A7** | |**D** |
Might win an Ocsar; you can't never tell.

|**A7** | |**D** |
The movies are gonna make me a big star,

|**E7** | |**A7** |
'Cause I can play the part so well.

Verse 3

‖**D** | |**G** | |
Well, I hope you come and see me in the movies,

D | |**A7** |
Then I know that you will plainly see

|**D** | |**G** |
The biggest fool that ever hit the big time,

|**A7** | |**D** | ‖
And all I gotta do is   act natural - ly.

Back Home Again

Words and Music by
John Denver

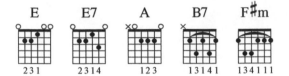

Verse 1

|E |E7 |A |
There's a storm   across the valley, clouds are rollin' in,

|B7 | |E |
The afternoon is heavy on your shoul - ders.

      |E |E7 |A |
There's a truck out on the four - lane a mile or more away,

|B7 | |E |
The whinin' of his wheels just makes it colder.

Verse 2

‖E |E7 |A |
He's an hour away from ridin' on your prayers up in the sky,

|B7 | |E |
And ten days on the road are barely gone.

    |E |E7 |A |
There's a fire softly burning, supper's on the stove,

     |B7 | |E | ‖
But it's the light in your eyes that makes him warm.

Chorus

A |B7 |E |E7 |A
Hey, it's good to be back home a-gain,

     |B7 |E |A
Sometimes this old farm feels   like a long-lost friend.

   |B7 | |E
Yes 'n' hey, it's good to be back home again.

Verse 3

```
      ‖E                |E7       |A                        |
      There's all the news to tell him, how'd you spend your time?

      |B7               |              |E          |
      And what's the latest thing the neighbors say?

            |E                |E7      |A                        |
      And your mother called last Friday, "Sunshine" made her cry,

            |B7               |              |E        |        ‖
      And you felt the baby move just yester-day.
```

Repeat Chorus

Interlude

```
      ‖A                |B7               |E          |A
      And oh, the time that I can lay this tired   old body down

      |F#m              |B7               |E          |E7
      And feel your fingers    feather soft up-on me.

       |A               |B7       |E                    |A
      The kisses that I live for, the love that lights my way,

      |F#m              |A        |B7                |
      The happiness that livin' with you brings me.
```

Verse 4

```
      ‖E                |E7       |A                        |
      It's the sweetest thing I know of, just spending time with you.

      |B7               |              |E        |
      It's the little things that make a house a home,

       |E       |E7      |A                       |
      Like a fire softly burning and supper on the stove

      |B7               |              |E        |        ‖
      And the light in your eyes that makes me warm.
```

Repeat Chorus (2X)

The Battle Hymn of Love

Words and Music by
Don Schlitz and Paul Overstreet

A   D   E

Intro

  A | D |A | |

  A | D |A |

Verse 1

‖A | | |

I will pledge my heart to the love we share,

|A |E |A |

Through the good and the bad times too.

|A | | |

I'll for - sake my rest for your happiness.

|A |E |A |

Till my death, I will stand by you.

Chorus 1

‖D | |A |

With God as my witness, this vow I will make:

|A | | |E

"To have and to hold you, no other to take."

|A | | |D

For rich or for poor, under skies gray or blue,

|A |E |A | | |

Till my death I will stand by you.

Verse 2

‖**A** | | |
There are wars and there are ru - mors, the wars yet to come,

|**A** |**E** |**A** |
Temp - tations we'll have to walk through.

|**A** | | |**D**
Though others may tremble, I will not run.

|**A** |**E** |**A** |
Till my death I will stand by you.

Chorus 2

‖**D** | |**A** |
I will put on the ar - mor of faithful - ness

|**A** | |**E** |
And fight for a heart that is true.

|**A** | | |**D**
Till the bat - tle is won I will not rest.

|**A** |**E** |**A** |
Till my death I will stand by you.

Chorus 3

‖**D** | |**A** |
With God as my witness, this vow I will make:

|**A** | | |**E**
"To have and to hold you, no other to take."

|**A** | | |**D**
For rich or for poor, under skies gray or blue,

|**A** |**E** |**A** |
Till my death I will stand by you.

|**A** | | |**D**
Till the bat - tle is won I will not run.

|**A** |**E** |**A** | ‖
Till my death I will stand by you.

Between the Devil and Me

Words and Music by
Carson Chamberlain and Harley Allen

D   G   Asus4   A

Intro   D | | | |

D | | |

Verse 1

‖**D** |

This world can take you by the hand

|**G** |

And tempt the soul of any man,

|**D**

But you can choose your path.

|**D** |**Asus4** |**A**

There's two roads you can take.

|**D** |

One way is right and one is wrong.

|**G** |

The flesh is weak but love is strong.

|**D**

And she's all I see

|**A**   **G** |**D** |

Between the devil and me.

Verse 2

  ‖**D** |
The gates of hell swing open wide,
  |**G** |
Inviting me to step in - side.
  |**D** |
"I'll be your friend," he calls a - gain;
  |**A** |
I know it's him.
  |**D** |
The flames are spreading everywhere,
  |**G** |
But through the smoke I see her there.
 |**D**
She's all I see
   |**A**   **G** |**D** | ‖
Between the devil and me.

Interlude   **D** |**A** |**D** |

Verse 3

  ‖**D** |
I hold her in my arms tonight.
  |**G** |
So safe and warm, I close my eyes.
 |**D**
And a cool breeze blows
  |**D** |**Asus4** |**A**
'Cross our bodies in the dark.
  |**D** |
Outside her reach is my concern.
  |**G** |
Somewhere I know a fire burns.
  |**D**
And she's all I see
  |**A**   **G** |**D** |
Between the devil and me.

Repeat Verse 2

Outro

      ‖**D** |
The gates of hell swing open wide,

     |**G** |
Invitin' me to stop in - side.

     |**D**
She's all I see

        |**A**   **G** |**D** | | **A** |**D**   ‖
Between the devil and me.

Big Red Sun Blues

Words and Music by
Lucinda Williams

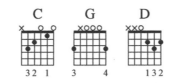

Intro

  C | |G | |

  D | |G |

Verse 1

      ||C |
Everything is going wrong;
       |G |
It's not right anymore.
       |D |
We can't seem to get along
       |G |
The way we did before.
      |C |
Sun is hanging in the sky,
      |G |
Sinking low and so am I,
        |D |
Just for the love of some - one,
      |G |
And a big red sun.

Chorus 1

‖**C** |
How'm I gonna lose

|**G** |
These big red sun   blues?

|**D** |
Big red sun,   big red sun,

|**G** |
Big red sun   blues.

Verse 2

‖**C** |
True love to hold

|**G** |
Is worth every‑thing.

|**D** |
It's worth more than gold

|**G** |
Or any diamond ring.

|**C** |
But this little diamond

|**G** |
And a heart that's been broken

|**D** |
Are all I got   from you,

|**G** |
Big red sun.

Repeat Chorus 1

Verse 3

```
                        ‖C              |
            Look  out  at  that  western  sky,
                     |G              |
            Out  over  the  open  plains.
                  |D           |
            God  only  knows  why
                          |G           |
            This  is  all  that  re - mains.
                              |C            |
            But  give  me  one  more  promise
                          |G         |
            And  another  kiss.
                       |D              |
            And  I  guess  the  deal's  still  on,
                       |G         |
            You  big  red  sun.
```

Repeat Chorus 1

Chorus 2

```
                        ‖C        |
            How'm  I  gonna  lose
                          |G          |
            These  big  red  sun   blues?
                    |D            |
            Big  red  sun,    big  red  sun,
                     |G      |        |D      |         |G      |        ‖
            Big  red  sun   blues.
```

Bigger Than the Beatles

Words and Music by
Steve Dukes and Jeb Anderson

G   D   C   Em

Verse 1

```
G              D       |C      D            |
He plays gui - tar      at a hotel bar

G              D       |Em      C          |
For out - of - towners and business men.

G              D       |C          D       |
He struts and sings to his  drum ma - chine,

    |G       D      |C    G          |
But he won't make it big at the Holiday Inn.

D                   |C      G          |
But she thinks that he looks like Elvis when he

C       G              |D           C     |
Runs his fin - gers through that jet - black hair.

D               |C    G          |
And sometimes she for - gets an order 'cause

    |C       G        |D              ||
She's so struck by him that she stops and stares.
```

Chorus

```
G              D      |C          D       |
They got a love big - ger than the Beatles,

G          D      |Em          C     |
Wild and free like a Rolling Stone.

G              D       |C       D       |
They got a love takes 'em higher than the Eagles.

G      D      |C
Ain't life such a sweet, sweet song!

G              D  |C             D  |G         D  |C       G       ||
Na, na, 'n, na, na,  na, na, 'n, na, na,   na, 'n na,  yeah, yeah, yeah.
```

Verse 2

```
       G           D       |C            D          |
    She pours some drinks,   loads up the sink

    G              D      |Em        C         |
    And dreams of being a movie star.

    G           D      |C              D              |
    Her mama said     she'd knock 'em dead,

    G           D         |C      G       |
    But Holly - wood hasn't called so   far.

    D                      |C          G                  |
    But he thinks she's as pretty as a picture when she

    C           G         |D              C    |
    Wipes down ta - bles in her apron strings.

    D                  |C      G        |
    And sometimes he for - gets a chorus 'cause

      |C          G              |D               ||
    She's shinin' like a beauty on the silver screen.
```

Repeat Chorus

Bridge

```
              ||Em                        |C
    No, you won't find their names on the Walk of Fame,

      |G                        |D
    But they ain't missing much.

                    |Em            |G    Em        |
    'Cause when the lights go down on tinsel town,

    C                    |D         |              ||
    All you need is a love,            ooh, hoo, hoo.
```

Repeat Chorus

A Boy Named Sue

Words and Music by
Shel Silverstein

G   C   D7

Verse 1

| **G** |
Well, my "daddy" left home when I was three,

| **C** |
And he didn't leave much to Ma and me,

| **D7** | | **G** |
Just this old guitar and an empty bottle of booze.

| **G** |
Now, I don't blame him because he run and hid,

| **C** | | **D7** |
But the meanest thing that he ever did was be - fore he left,

| **D7** | **G** |
He went and named me Sue.

Verse 2

|| **G** |
Well, he must have thought it was quite a joke,

| **C** |
And it got lots of laughs from a lot of folks.

| **D7** | | **G** |
It seems I had to fight my whole life through.

| **G** |
Some gal would giggle and I'd get red.

| **C** |
And some guy would laugh and I'd bust his head,

| **D7** | | **G** |
I tell you, life ain't easy for a boy named Sue.

Verse 3

      ‖**G** |

Well, I grew up quick and I grew up mean.

    |**C** | |

My fist got hard and my wits got keen.

D7 | |**G** |

Roamed from town to town to hide my shame.

    |**G** | |

But I made me a vow to the moon and stars,

C |

I'd search the honky - tonks and bars

   |**D7** | |**G** |

And kill that man that give me that awful name.

Verse 4

     ‖**G** |

But it was Gatlinburg in mid July,

     |**C** | |

And I had just hit town and my throat was dry.

D7 | |**G** |

  I'd thought I'd stop and have myself a brew.

   |**G** | |

At an old saloon on a street of mud,

C | |

There at a table dealing stud

D7 | |**G** |

Sat the dirty, mangy dog that named me Sue.

Verse 5

```
  ‖G                          |
Well, I knew that snake was my own sweet dad
     |C                       |
From a worn-out picture that my mother had.
   |D7                |              |G         |
And I knew that scar on his cheek and his evil eye.
     |G                |
He was big and bent and gray and old
   |C                  |
And I looked at him and my blood ran cold,
   |D7             |        |G           |
And I said "My name is Sue.    How do you do?
  |G              |      |      |                    |       |
Now you're gonna die."          Yeah that's what I told him.
```

Verse 6

```
   ‖G                    |              |
Well, I hit him hard right be - tween the eyes and
C                        |         |
  He went down, But to my surprise
D7                     |           |G         |
  He come up with a knife and cut off a piece of my ear.
   |G               |
But I busted a chair right a - cross his teeth,
    |C                  |              |
And we crashed through the wall and into the street,
D7                    |                   |G     |
Kicking and a-gouging in the mud and the blood and the beer.
```

Verse 7

```
|‖G                      |                    |
I tell you I've fought tougher men but I

C                    |
Really can't remember when.

   |D7                          |                    |G           |
He kicked like a mule and he bit like a croco - dile.

   |G                      |
I heard him laugh and then I heard him cuss,

      |C                       |
And he went for his gun and I pulled mine first.

   |D7                       |                  |G        |
He stood there looking at me      and I saw him smile.
```

Verse 8

```
              |‖G           |          |                      |
And he said, "Son,        this world is rough and if a man's gonna make it,

   |G                    |                      |D7              |G      |
He's gotta be tough, and I know I wouldn't be there to help you a - long.

   |G                    |
So I give you that name and I said goodbye,

   |C                       |
I knew you'd have to get tough    or die.

   |D7                      |                      |G           |
And it's that name that helped to make you strong."
```

Verse 9

```
      |‖G              |                  |
Yeah,    he said, "Now, you just fought one helluva fight,

      |C                       |
And I know you hate me and you've got the right

   |D7                   |                      |G        |
To kill me now and I wouldn't blame you if you do.

      |G                    |
But you ought to thank me be - fore I die

      |C                       |
For the gravel in your guts and the spit in your eye

      |D7                   |              |G        |
'Cause I'm the son of a bitch that named you Sue."

      |G              |                  |C
Yeah, what could I do?    What could I do?
```

Verse 10

```
          || C                      | D7
I got all choked up and I threw down my gun

          | D7                    | G                      |
And called him my pa and he called me his son,

G                                      |                      |          | D7
   And I come away with a different point of view.

          | G              |
And I think about him now and then.

          | C              |          | D7 N.C.
Every time I tried, every time I win,      and if I ever have a son

N.C.                                                              | G      ||
I think I'm gonna name him ... Bill or George! ... anything but Sue!
```

The Call of the Wild

Words and Music by
Aaron Tippin, Buddy Brock
and Michael Heeney

E7   A   B   G

Intro | E7 | | |

Verse 1

||E7 | | |
She's been star - ing out the window four nights   in a row.

|E7 | | |
Like a caged - up tiger, she's a - pacing the floor.

|A | | |
Oh, the night is young and the moon is full,

|E7 | | |
And she just can't resist when she feels the pull.

|B |
She's got a restless spirit that she can't control,

|A | |B |
And when she gets like this, I gotta let her go.

Chorus 1

‖**E7** | | |
She hears the call of the wild every once   in a while.

|**E7** |
She lets down her hair, she's gotta get somewhere.

|**E7** |
She can turn it loose and howl.

|**A** |
I know what's in store; Katie, bar the door

|**A** |
When she winks at me and smiles.

|**E7** |
She's in a foot-stomping, honky-tonking,

E7 |**A** |
Love-making state of mind.

|**G** |**A**   **B**   **G** |**E7** | | .
So ex‑cuse me, y'all, I gotta answer the call of the wild.

|

Verse 2

‖**E7** | | |
If there's ev‑er been a lady, well, baby is

|**E7** | | |
Just more   of a woman at times like this.

|**A** | | |
Now, don't you worry 'bout baby stepping out of line.

|**E7** | | |
Yeah, she drives   me crazy, but it suits me fine.

|**B** |
'Cause she's hard to handle, so I hold on tight,

|**A** | |**B** |
And Lord knows I got my hands full tonight.

Repeat Chorus 1

Interlude   **G** |**A**   **B**   **G** |**E7** |

26

Chorus 2

         ‖**E7** | | |
Oh, she hears the call of the wild every once   in a while.

     |**E7** |
She lets down her hair, she's gotta get somewhere.

     |**E7** |
She can turn it loose and howl.

    |**A** |
I know what's in store; Katie, bar the door

     |**A** |
When she winks at me and smiles.

      |**E7** |
She's in a foot-stomping, honky-tonking,

E7 |**A** |
Love-making state of mind.

    |**G** |**A**   **B** **G** |**E7** |
So ex - cuse me, y'all, I gotta answer the call of the wild.

    |**G**
I said, pardon me, y'all,

    |**A**   **B** **G** |**E7** | | | ‖
I gotta answer the call of the wild.

Cold, Cold Heart

Words and Music by
Hank Williams

E   B7   E7   A

Verse 1

|E | | |B7
I tried so hard, my dear, to show that you're my every dream.

|B7 | | |E
Yet you're afraid each thing I do is just some evil scheme.

|E | |E7 |A
A memory from your lonesome past keeps us so far a - part.

|B7 | | |E
Why can't I free your doubtful mind and melt your cold, cold heart?

Verse 2

‖E | | |B7
An - other love be - fore my time made your heart sad and blue.

|B7 | | |E
And so my heart is paying now for things I didn't do.

|E | |E7 |A
In anger unkind words are said that make the teardrops start.

|B7 | | |E
Why can't I free your doubtful mind and melt your cold, cold heart?

Verse 3

```
       ||E                  |                 |              |B7
       You'll never know how much it hurts to see you sit and cry.

       |B7                  |                 |              |E
       You know you need and want my love, yet you're afraid to try.

       |E           |hide from life? To|E7         |A
       Why do you run and hide from life? To try it just ain't smart.

       |B7                 |                 |              |E
       Why can't I free your doubtful mind and melt your cold, cold heart?
```

Verse 4

```
       ||E                  |                 |              |B7
       There was a time when I believed that you belonged to me.

       |B7                 |                 |         |E
       But now I know your heart is shackled to a memo - ry.

       |E           |                 |E7         |A
       The more I learn to care for you the more we drift a - part.

       |B7                 |                 |              |E        ||
       Why can't I free your doubtful mind and melt your cold, cold heart.
```

Don't Let Our Love Start Slippin'

Words and Music by
Pete Wasner and Vince Gill

G   A   D

Intro

| G | | A | D | | | |

| G | | A | D | | |

Verse 1

‖ D | |
We've been up

| G | |
All night long,

| A | |
Trying to solve a problem

| D | |
Till it's almost dawn.

| D | |
Ain't no time for sleeping

| G | |
If our love is wearing thin.

| A | |
'Cause I ain't giving up

| D | |
And you ain't giv - ing in.

Chorus

‖**G** |
Don't let our love start slipping,

A |**D** |
Love start slipping away.

|**G**
'Cause the life   we've been living

|**A** |**D** |
Gets harder every day.

|**G** |
Don't let our love start slipping,

A |**D** |
Love start slipping away.

Verse 2

‖**D** |
A wounded love

|**G** |
Walks a real thin   line,

|**A** |
And no communi - cation

|**D** |
Will kill it ev - 'ry time.

|**D** |
So open up   your heart;

|**G** |
Baby, we can work   it out.

|**A** |
'Cause we've got the kind of love

|**D** |
People dream   about.

Repeat Chorus

Bridge

```
A                           |G          |
    It's past the point of right or wrong.
A                      |G       |       ||
    Let's find a way to just hold on.
```

Interlude

```
G            |A          |D          |          |

G            |A          |D      |
```

Repeat Chorus

Outro

```
                   ||G          |
    Don't let our love start slipping,
A                  |D       |        |
    Love start slipping away.
G          |A          |D      |          |

G          |A          |D      |          ||
```

Folsom Prison Blues

Words and Music by
John R. Cash

D   G   C

Intro

| D | | | G | |

Verse 1

‖ G | |
I hear the train a - coming;

| G | |
It's rolling 'round the bend,

| G | |
And I ain't seen the sunshine

| G | |
Since I don't know when.

| C | | |
I'm stuck in Folsom Prison,

C | | G | | | |
And time keeps dragging on.

| D | | |
But that train keeps a - rolling

D | | G | |
On down to San An - tone.

Verse 2

    ‖**G** |

When I was just a baby,

  |**G** | |

My mama told me, "Son,

G |

Always be a good boy;

   |**G** |

Don't ever play with guns."

     |**C** | |

But I shot a man in Reno

C | |**G** | | |

  Just to watch him die.

      |**D** | |

When I hear that whistle blowing,

D | |**G** |

  I hang my head and cry.

Verse 3

    ‖**G** |

I bet there's rich folks eating

     |**G** |

In a fancy dining car.

     |**G** |

They're probably drinking coffee

    |**G** |

And smoking big ci - gars.

     |**C** | |

But I know I had it coming;

C | |**G** | | |

  I know I can't be free.

     |**D** | |

But those people keep a - moving

D | |**G** |

  And that's what tortures me.

Verse 4

```
         ‖G                    |
Well, if they freed me from this prison,
          |G               |
If that railroad train was mine,
 |G               |            |
I bet I'd move it on a little
G                |         |
Farther down the line.
C                |        |
Far from Folsom Prison,
C                    |       |G     |        |          |
   That's where I want to stay.
         |D                |         |
And I'd let that lonesome whistle
D         |       |G    |     |D    |      |G    |         ‖
   Blow my blues a-way.
```

Down on the Farm

Words and Music by
Kerry Kurt Phillips and Jerry Laseter

A   D7   E7

Verse 1

A
Ev'ry Friday night there's a steady cloud of dust

| **A**
That leads back to a field filled with pickup trucks.

| **D7**
Got old Hank crankin'   way up loud,

| **A**
Got cool - ers in the back,   tail - gates down.

| **E7**
There's a big fire burnin' but don't   be alarmed

| **A**
It's just coun - try boys and girls gettin'   down on the farm.

Verse 2

|| **A**
Ed's   been on a tractor, ain't seen Becky all week;

| **A**
Somebod - y said they'd seen 'em headed down to the creek.

| **D7**
Farm - er Johnson's daughter just pulled up in a Jeep.

| **A**
Man, he knows how to grow 'em, if you know what I mean.

| **E7**
Ol' Dave's gettin' loud but he don't   mean no harm.

| **A**
We're just coun - try boys and girls gettin' down on the farm.

Chorus

|| **D7** |
You can have a lot of fun   in a New York minute,

| **A** |
But there's some   things you can't do inside those   city limits.

| **E7** |
Ain't   no closin' time,   ain't   no cover charge,

| **A** | |
Just coun - try boys and girls gettin' down on the farm.

A | | |

Verse 3

|| **A** |
Well, you can come as you are,   there ain't no dress code,

| **A** |
Just some rural route rules that you   need to know.

| **D7** |
Don't mess with the bull,   he can get real mean.

| **A** |
Don't for - get to shut the gate;   stay out of the beans.

| **E7** |
If   it starts to rainin' we'll just head out to the barn.

| **A** | | |
We're coun - try boys and girls gettin' down on the farm.

Repeat Chorus

Tag

| **E7** |
Ain't   no closin' time, ain't   no cover charge,

| **A** | ||
Just coun - try boys and girls gettin' down on the farm.

Forever and Ever, Amen

Words and Music by
Paul Overstreet and Don Schlitz

D   G   E   A

Intro   **D** | | |

Verse 1

‖**D** |**G** |**D** |
You may think that I'm   talking fool - ish.

|**G** | |**D** |
You've heard that I'm wild   and I'm free.

|**G** | |**D** |
You may wonder how   I can promise you now

|**E** | |**A** |
This love that I feel   for you al - ways will be.

|**D** |**G** |**D** |
But you're not just time   that I'm kill - ing.

|**G** | |**D** |
I'm no longer one   of those guys.

|**G** | |**D** |
As sure as I live,   this love that I give

|**E** | |**A** | ‖
Is gonna be yours   until the day that I die.   Oh, baby,

Chorus

```
         D          |G        |D        |
I'm gonna love    you forev - er,
       |G          |         |D        |
For - ever and ev - er, amen,
      |G           |         |D        |
As long as old men    sit and talk about the weath - er,
     |E            |         |A        |
As long as old wom - en sit and talk about old men.
        |D         |G       |D        |
If you wonder how long    I'll be faith - ful,
       |G          |         |E        |    |
I'll be happy to tell   you again.
G          |A       |D        |G        |
I'm gonna love   you for - ever and ev - er,
     |E          |A       |D        |         ||
For - ever and ev - er, a - men.
```

Interlude

```
G    |A    |D    |G    |E    |A    |D    |
```

Verse 2

```
              ||D         |G        |D        |
They say time takes its toll    on a bod - y.
            |G            |         |D        |
Makes the young girls brown   hair turn gray.
      |G                  |         |D        |
Well, honey, I don't care;  I ain't in love with your hair,
         |E              |         |A        |
And if it all fell out,    well, I'd love you anyway.
           |D             |G        |D        |
They say time can play tricks    on a mem - 'ry,
         |G              |         |D        |
Make people forget   things they knew.
           |G          |    |D        |
Well, it's easy to see    it's happening to me.
             |E          |         |A        |         ||
I've al - ready forgot - ten every woman but you.    Oh, darling,
```

Repeat Chorus

The Gambler

Words and Music by
Don Schlitz

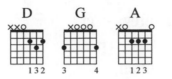

Verse 1

|D | |G |D
On a warm summer's eve - nin' on a train bound for no - where,

|D | | |A
I met up with the gam - bler; we were both too tired to sleep.

|D | |G |D
So we took turns star - in' out the window at the dark - ness

|G |D |A |D
Till boredom overtook us   and he began to speak.

Verse 2

‖D | |G |D
He said, "Son I've made a life   out of readin' people's fac - es

|D | | |A
And knowin' what their cards were   by the way they held their eyes.

|D | |G |D
And if you don't mind my say - in', I can see you're out of ac - es.

|G |D |A |D |
For a taste of your whis - key   I'll give you some advice."

Verse 3

‖D | |G |D |
So I handed him my bot - tle and he drank down my last swallow.

D | | |A
Then he bummed a cig - arette and asked me for a light.

|D | |G |D
And the night got deathly qui - et, and his face lost all expres - sion.

|G |D |A |D
Said, "If you're gonna play the game, boy, ya gotta learn to play it right.

Chorus

    ||**D** | |
You got to know when to hold 'em,

G |**D** |
Know when to fold 'em,

G |**D** | |**A**
Know when to walk away and know when to run.

    |**D** | |**G** |**D**
You never count your money when you're sittin' at the ta - ble.

    |**D** **G** |**D** |
There'll be time e - nough for count - in'

A |**D** | ||
When the dealin's done.

Verse 4

D | |**G** |**D**
Ev'ry gambler knows that the secret to surviv - in'

|**D** | |**A**
Is knowing what to throw away and knowin' what to keep,

|**D** | |**G** |**D**
'Cause ev'ry hand's a win - ner and ev'ry hand's a los - er,

|**G** |**D** |**A** |**D**
And the best that you can hope for is to die in your sleep."

Verse 5

||**D** | |**G** |**D** |
And when he'd finished speakin', he turned back towards the win - dow,

D | | |**A**
Crushed out his cigarette and faded off to sleep.

|**D** | |**G** |**D**
And somewhere in the dark - ness the gambler, he broke even.

|**G** |**D** |**A** |**D**
But in his final words I found an ace that I could keep.

Repeat Chorus

I Just Want to Dance with You

Words and Music by
Roger Cook and John Prine

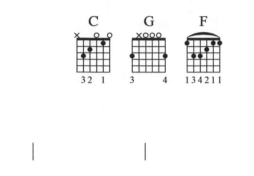

Intro   C | | | ||

Verse 1

C | |
I don't want to be the kind to hesitate,
C |G |
Be too shy, way too late.
G
I don't care what they say other lovers do,
 |G |C
I just want to dance with you.
 |C
I got a feeling that you have a heart like mine,
 |C |G
So let it show, let it shine.
 |G
If we have a chance to make one heart of two,
 |G |C
Then I just want to dance with you.

                                          ‖**F** |
Chorus 1   I want to dance with you,
                                             |**C**
                  Twirl you all a-round the floor.
                          |**C** |**G**
                  That's what they intended dancing for,
                     |**G** |**C** |
                  And I   just want to dance with you.
                              |**F** |
                  I want to dance with you,
                  F |**C**
                    Hold you in my arms once more.
                      |**C** |**G**
                  That's what they invented dancing for,
                     |**G** |**C** |
                  And I   just want to dance with you.

                                          ‖**C** | |
Verse 2   I caught you looking at me when I looked at you,
                  C |**G**
                  Yes, I did. Now ain't that true?
                     |**G** |
                  You   won't get embarrassed by the things I do;
                   |**G** |**C**
                  I   just want to dance with you.
                         |**C** | |
                  Oh, the boys are playing softly and the girls are too;
                  C |**G**
                  So am I and so are you.
                    |**G** |
                  If   this was a movie, we'd be right on cue,
                     |**G** |**C**
                  And I   just want to dance with you.

Repeat Chorus 1

Interlude   C | | |G |

               G | | |C

                        ‖F |
Chorus 2   I want to dance with you,
                        |C
               Twirl you all a‑round the floor.
                  |C |G
               That's what they invented dancing for,
                  |G |C |
               And I   just want to dance with you.
                     |F |
               I want to dance with you,
               F |C
                 Hold you in my arms once more.
                  |C |G
               That's what they intended dancing for,
                  |G |C
               And I   just want to dance with you.
               |G |C   ‖
               I   just want to dance with you.

44

Kiss an Angel Good Mornin'

Words and Music by
Ben Peters

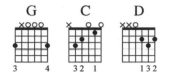

Verse 1

|**G** | **|C** |
When - ever I chance to meet   some old friends on the street,

|**D** | **|G** |
They wonder how does a man get to be this way.

|**G** | **|C** |
I've always got a smilin' face,   any time and any place,

|**D** | **|G** |
And ev'ry time they ask me why, I just smile and say:

Chorus

‖**G**   **|D** |
You've got to kiss an angel good mornin'

|**C** | **G** | |
And let her know you think about her when you're gone.

G   **|D** |
Kiss an angel good mornin'

|**C** | **G** | |
And love her like the devil when you get back home.

Verse 2

‖**G** | **|C** |
Well, people may try to guess the secret of happiness,

|**D** | **|G** |
But some of them never learn that it's a simple thing.

|**G** | **|C** |
The secret I'm speakin' of   is a woman and man in love,

|**D** | **|G** |
And the answer is in the song that I always sing.

Repeat Chorus

I Like It, I Love It

Words and Music by
Steve Dukes, Markus Anthony Hall
and Jeb Anderson

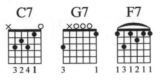

Verse 1

|C7 | | |
Spent forty - eight dollars last night at the county fair.

|C7 | |G7 |
I throwed out my shoulder but I won her that teddy bear.

|F7 |
She's got me sayin' sugar pie, honey, darlin', and dear.

|C7 |
I ain't seen the Braves play a game all year.

|G7 |
I'm gonna get fired if I don't get some sleep.

|G7 |
My long lost buddies say I'm gettin' in too deep.

Chorus

||C7 |
But I like it, I love it, I want some more of it.

|F7 |
I try so hard, I can't rise above it.

|G7 |
I don't know what it is 'bout that little gal's lovin',

|C7   N.C. |
But I like it,   I love it, I want some more of it.

Verse 2

||**C7** | | |
My mama and daddy tried to teach me courtesy,

|**C7** | |**G7** |
But it never sank in till that girl got a hold of me.

|**F7** |
Now I'm holdin' up umbrellas and openin' up doors,

|**C7** |
I'm takin' out trash and I'm sweepin' my floor.

|**G7** |
I'm crossin' my fingers and countin' every kiss,

|**G7** |
And prayin' that it keeps on goin' on like this,

||**C7**
Repeat Chorus   'Cause I like it, I love it, *etc.*

||**F7** |
Bridge   Gotta wash my truck   and dress up

|**C7** |
To pick her up to watch TV.

|**F7** |
If she sits down on the sofa,   she'll move a little closer.

|**G7** |
She can't get enough of me.

||**C7**
Repeat Chorus   And I like it, I love it, *etc.*

I Will...But

Words and Music by
Kristyn Osborn and Jason Deere

D   A   G   Bm

Intro

D   A |G   A |
I won't be bored;

D   A |G   A |
I won't be ignored.   *Hey!*

D   A |G   A |D   A |G   A ||

Verse 1

D   A |G   A |
I won't be your dirt - y se - cret.

D   A |G   A |
I won't be your cure - all pill.

D   A |G   A |
And I won't run to fetch the wa - ter

D   A |G   A ||
Just to tum - ble down the hill.

Verse 2

D   A |G   A |
I won't be your Fri - day pay - check.

D   A |G   A |
I won't be the prize you flaunt.

D   A |G   A |
And I won't be your Mar - tha Stew - art, baby,

D   A |G   A
Or your all - night res - taurant.

Chorus 1

```
        ‖D      A    |G        A            |
But I will,   I will,  I will  be your ev - erything
 D       A          |G          A
  (If you   make me feel  like a wom - an should).
     |D      A    |G          A            |
I will,  I will,  I will  be the whole  shebang.
Bm          A     |G    A      ‖
   You know  I will.        But
```

Verse 3

```
 D        A            |G      A    |
  I won't  be your crutch  to lean  on.
 D        A        |G       A     |
  I won't   wear sti - letto heels.
 D        A          |G        A        |
  I won't  walk a mile  in your    shoes
 D        A         |G      A      ‖
  Just so I   know how   it feels.
```

Verse 4

```
 D        A          |G    A      |
  I won't  be your ob - liga - tion.
 D        A          |G         A      |
  I won't  be your Bar - bie doll.
 D        A          |G       A      |D
  I won't  be the por - trait of  perfec - tion
  A       |G       A
To  adorn   your wall.
```

Repeat Chorus 1

49

Bridge

      D   A |G   A |D   A
    Hey,   you know, you know I will.

  |G   A |D   A |G   A |D   A |G   A   ‖
All right.

Verse 5

D N.C. | |
I won't be your life - time girlfriend.

D N.C. | |
I won't be just one of the guys.

D N.C. |
I won't be your ma - ma's favorite.

     |G   N.C. |G   N.C.
I re - fuse to be   the last in   line.

Chorus 2

              ‖D   A |G   A |
But I will, I will, I will be your ev - erything

D   A |G   A
 (If you make me feel like a wom - an should).

    |D   A |G   A |
I will, I will, I will be the whole shebang.

Bm   A |G   A
You know I will.

Outro

```
        ‖D    A    |G        A        |
Yeah, I will,  I will,  I will  be your ev - erything.
D      A      |G        A        |
 I will,  I will  be the whole  shebang.
D      A      |G        A        |
 I will,  I will  be your ev - erything.
D      A        |G      A |D    A  |G    A    |
 I will,   I will,   I will,  I will,       yeah.
D          A        |G              A      |
  You know  I will, you know, you know I will.
D          A        |G              A      |
  You know  I will, you know, you know I will,
D    A   |G    A    |D    A   |G    A    |D        ‖
Yeah.
```

Jambalaya
(On the Bayou)

Words and Music by
Hank Williams

C G

Verse 1

||C | |G |
Goodbye Joe, me gotta go, me oh my oh.

|G | |C |
Me gotta go pole the pirogue down the bayou.

|C | |G |
My Y - vonne, the sweetest one, me oh my oh.

|G | |C |
Son of a gun, we'll have big fun on the bayou.

Chorus

||C | |G |
Jamba - laya and a crawfish pie and filé gumbo,

|G | |C |
'Cause to - night I'm gonna see my ma cher a - mio.

|C | |G |
Pick gui - tar, fill fruit jar, and be gay-o.

|G | |C |
Son of a gun, we'll have big fun on the bayou.

Verse 2

    ‖ **C** | | **G** |
Thibo - deaux, Fontain - eaux, the place is buzzing.
    | **G** | | **C** |
Kinfolk come to see Y - vonne by the dozen.
    | **C** | | **G** |
Dress in style, go hog - wild, me oh my oh.
     | **G** | | **C** |
Son of a gun, we'll have big fun on the bayou.

Chorus

    ‖ **C** | | **G** |
Jamba - laya and a crawfish pie and filé gumbo,
     | **G** | | **C** |
'Cause to - night I'm gonna see my ma cher a - mio.
    | **C** | | **G** |
Pick gui - tar, fill fruit jar, and be gay-o.
    | **G** | | **C** | ‖
Son of a gun, we'll have big fun on the bayou.

Jolene

Words and Music by
Dolly Parton

Em   G   D/F#   D

Intro   Em | | |

Chorus

‖Em   G |D/F# |Em
Jo - lene, Jo - lene, Jo - lene, Jo - lene,

|D |Em |
I'm begging of you, please don't take my man.

|Em   G |D/F# |Em |
Jo - lene, Jo - lene, Jo - lene, Jo - lene,

D |Em |
Please don't take him just because you can.

Verse 1

‖Em   G
Your beauty is be - yond compare,

|D/F#   Em
With flaming locks of auburn hair,

|D |Em |
With ivory skin and eyes of emerald green.

|Em   G
Your smile is like a breath of spring,

|D/F#   Em
Your voice is soft like summer rain,

|D |Em |
And I cannot compete with you,   Jolene.

Verse 2

```
  ‖ Em                  G
  He talks about you in his sleep,
         | D/F♯           Em
  And there's nothing I can do to keep
    | D                              | Em        |
  From crying when he calls your name, Jolene.
    | Em          G
  And I can easily understand
    | D/F♯              Em
  How you could easily take my man,
        | D                          | Em        |
  But you don't know what he means to me, Jo - lene.
```

Repeat Chorus

Verse 3

```
  Em                    G
  You could have your choice of men,
    | D/F♯          Em            |
  But I could never love again.
  D                         | Em        |
  He's the only one for me, Jo - lene.
   | Em             G
  I had to have this talk with you;
     | D/F♯           Em
  My happiness de - pends on you
        | D                       | Em        |
  And what - ever you decide to do, Jo - lene.
```

Repeat Chorus

Outro

```
  ‖ Em      |        |        |        ‖
  Jo - lene, Jo - lene.
```

A Little Less Talk and a Lot More Action

Words and Music by
Keith Hinton and Jimmy Alan Stewart

A   D   E

Intro   **A** | | |

Verse 1

‖ **A** | |
Well, I was getting kind of tired of her   endless chatter;

A |
Nothing I could say ever seemed to matter.

|**D** |
So, I took a little drive just to clear my head;

|**A** |
I saw a flashing neon   up ahead.

|**E** |
It looked like a place to find some   satisfaction,

|**A**   **N.C.** | ‖
With a little less talk and a lot more action.

Interlude 1   **A** | | |

Verse 2

```
          ‖A                                          |
I paid the man at the door and pushed my way to the bar;
   |A                       |
I shouted for a drink over a screaming guitar.
   |D                    |
A drunk on a stool tried to mess with my head,
      |A                    |
But I didn't even listen to a  word he said.
   |E                    |
I knew somewhere amid all   this distraction
         |A     N.C.         |
Was a little less talk and a lot more action.
```

Chorus

```
   ‖D              |
A little less talk,   if you please;
   |A                  |
A lot more loving is-a  what I need.
      |E                 |
Let's get on down to the main attraction
        |A     N.C.            |                    ‖
With a little less talk and a lot more action.
```

Interlude 2

```
A              |           |           |           |

D              |           |A          |           |

E              |           |A          |
```

Verse 3

```
            ‖A                        |
Yes, she was fighting them off at a  corner table;
          | A                |
She had a long-neck bottle, she was peeling the label.
        | D                    |
The look on her face, it was perfectly clear;
            | A                    |
She said,   "Somebody, please get me   out of here."
          | E                      |
The look she shot me through the glass refraction
          | A      N.C.        |
Said a little less talk and a lot more action.
```

Repeat Chorus

Outro

```
        ‖ D            |
A little less talk,
    | A              |
A lot more action.
          | E                      |
Let's get on down to the main attraction
          | A                |                  |
With a little less talk and a lot more action.
E                      |                   | A    N.C.      |       A |
Get on down to the main attraction with a little less talk
A                          |           ‖
    And a lot more action.
```

Love Gets Me Every Time

Words and Music by
Shania Twain and R.J. Lange

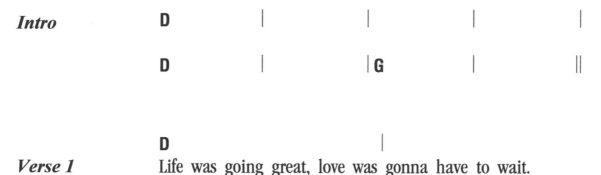

Intro

D | | | |

D | |G | ||

Verse 1

D |
Life was going great, love was gonna have to wait.

|G |
Was in no hurry, had no worries.

|D |
Staying single was the plan, didn't need a steady man.

|G |
I had it covered till I dis - covered

Chorus 1

    ‖**A** |**G**
That love gets me every time.

    |**A** |**G**
My heart changed my mind.

  |**G** **N.C.** |
I gol' darn gone and done it.

        |**G** |
Gone and done it. (Gone and done it.)

            |**D** |
I guess I fell in love. (Gone and done it.)

          |**G** |
Must've been the way he walked. (Gone and done it.)

         |**D** |
Or his sweet, sweet talk. (Gone and done it.)

      |**A** |**G** |
I guess I

G | **N.C.** | ‖
Gol' darn gone   and done it.   Ooh!

Interlude 1   **D** | |**G** | ‖

Verse 2

D |
I was quite content, just a - paying my own rent.

      |**G** |
It was my place; I needed my space.

      |**D** |
I was free to shop around, in no rush to settle down.

       |**G** |
I had it covered till I dis - covered

Repeat Chorus

Interlude 2 D | |G | |

Chorus 2

||**A** |**G**
Well, love gets me every time.

|**A** |**G**
My heart changed my mind.

|**G** **N.C.** |
And I gol' darn gone and done it.

|**G** |
Gone and done it. (Gone and done it.)

|**D** |
Guess I fell in love. (Gone and done it.)

|**G** |
Must've been the way he walked. (Gone and done it.)

|**D** |
Or his sweet, sweet talk. (Gone and done it.)

|**G** |
It's in the way he calls my name. (Gone and done it.)

|**D** |
And I know I'll never be the same. (Gone and done it.)

|**A** |**G**
Don't you know that love gets me every time.

|**A** |**G**
My heart changed my mind.

|**G** | | **N.C.** | ||
I gol' darn gone and done it.

Outro

D | |**G** |
Thought I had it covered. Aha.

G |**D** |
Life was going great.

|**G** | ||
Well, I gol' darn gone and done it.

61

Me and Bobby McGee

Words and Music by
Kris Krisofferson and Fred Foster

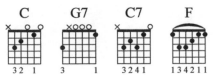

Verse 1

C | | | |
Busted flat in Baton Rouge,   headin' for the trains,

C | |G7 | |
Feelin' nearly faded as my jeans.

G7 | | | |
   Bobby thumbed a diesel down   just before it rained,

G7 | |C | |
   Took us all the way to New Orleans.

C | | |
I took my har-poon out of my dirty red ban-dana

|C |C7 |F |
And was blowin' sad while Bobby sang the blues.

|F | |C |
With them windshield wipers slappin' time and Bobby clappin' hands,

|G7 | |C | ||
We finally sang up every song that driver knew.

Chorus 1

F | |C | |
   Freedom's just an-other word for nothin' left to lose.

G7 | |C | |
Nothin' ain't worth nothin', but it's free.

F | |C | |
   Feelin' good was easy, Lord, when   Bobby sang the blues,

G7 | | | |
   And feelin' good was good enough for me,

G7 | |C |
   Good enough for me and Bobby Mc-Gee.

Verse 2

```
   ||C              |              |              |          |
From  the  coal  mines  of  Ken - tucky    to  the  California  sun,

C                    |              |G7            |          |
Bobby  shared  the  secrets  of  my  soul.

G7                          |              |          |       |
       Standin'  right  be - side  me,  Lord,  through     everything  I  done,

G7                          |                    |C         |
   And  every  night  she  kept  me  from  the  cold.

     |C                |              |          |       |
Then  somewhere  near  Sa - linas,  Lord,  I  let  her  slip  a - way,

C              |C7            |F              |
Lookin'  for  the  home  I  hope  she'll  find.

             |F            |              |C         |        |
And  I'd  trade  all  of  my  to - morrows  for  a  single  yester - day,

G7                  |              |C         |          ||
Holdin'  Bobby's  body  next  to  mine.
```

Chorus 2

```
F                        |              |C         |          |
       Freedom's  just  an - other  word  for  nothin'  left  to  lose.

G7                        |              |C         |       |
   Nothin'  left  is  all  she  left  for  me.

F                        |              |C              |      |
   Feelin'  good  was  easy,  Lord,  when     Bobby  sang  the blues,

G7                        |              |         |        |
   And,  buddy,  that  was  good  enough  for  me,

G7                        |              |C         |        ||
   Good  enough  for  me  and  Bobby  Mc - Gee.
```

Meat & Potato Man

Written by John Pennell
and Harley Allen

A   D   E   Dm

  1 2 3   1 3 2   2 3 1   2 3 1

Interlude   **A** |**D** |**A** | |

    E | |**A** |**E**

    ‖**A** |**D** |

Verse 1   I like my steak well done,   my taters fried,

    A |

    Football games on Monday night.

    |**E**

It's just who I am,

    |**E** |**A** |**E**

A meat and potato man.

    ‖**A** |**D** |

Verse 2   I like my coffee black, ol'   TV shows,

    A |

    My women hot, and my beer ice cold.

    |**E**

It's just who I am,

    |**E** |**A** |

A meat and potato man.

Bridge 1

     ‖**D** |**Dm** |
I don't like caviar,   sushi bars,

A |
 The IRS, or phony stars.

   |**E**
I'm a Haggard fan,

 |**E** |**A** |**E**   ‖
A meat and potato man.

Interlude   **A** |**D**   **A** | |

          E | **A** |**E**

Verse 3

      ‖**A** |**D** |
I like my fishing holes, lightning bugs,

A |
 Flatt 'n' Scruggs, and my woman's love.

   |**E**
It's just who I am,

 |**E** |**A** |**E**
A meat and potato man.

Verse 4

      ‖**A** |**D** |
I like my Wrangler jeans, cowboy boots,

A |
 Cornbread and beans, and country roots.

   |**E**
It's just who I am,

 |**E** |**A** |
A meat and potato man.

Bridge 2

```
              ‖D          |Dm                |
I don't like  politics,       hypocrites,
A                               |
  Folks with poodles dressed  like kids.
      |E
I'm a hound dog fan,
  |E                      |A              |
A meat and potato man.
              |E
Yeah, that's just   what I am,
  |E                      |A          |            ‖
A meat and potato man.
```

The Night's Too Long

Words and Music by
Lucinda Williams

A   D   E

Intro   **A** | | | ||

Verse 1

A |
Sylvia was work - ing

|**D** |
As a wait - ress in Beau - mont.

|**A** |
She said, "I'm moving away,

|**A** |**E**
I'm gonna get what I want.

|**A** |
I'm tired of these small - town boys;

|**D** |
They don't move fast e - nough.

|**A** |
I'm gonna find me one who wears a leather jacket

|**E** |**A** |
And likes his living rough."

Verse 2

```
          ‖A                |
So she saved her tips and overtime
        |D                 |
And bought an old rusty car.
       |A                  |
She sold most everything   she had
      |A              |E
To make a brand-new start.
              |A           |
She said, "I won't be needing these
              |D           |
Silly dress - es and nylon hose,
                |A              |
'Cause when I   get to where I'm go - ing,
             |E                   |A          |
I'm gonna buy me all new clothes."
```

Chorus

```
                    ‖D        |
The night's too long;
D            |A            |
  It just drags on and on.
A                            |E       |
  And then there's never enough;
E                        |A           |
  That's when the sun starts coming up.
A               |D        |
  Don't let go of her hand;
E                    |A       |D
  You just might be the right    man.
    |E          |D
She loves the night;
    |E              |D
She loves the night.
    |E                    |D              |A        |
She doesn't want the night,  don't want it to end.
D            |A       |D
  Don't want it to end.
```

Verse 3

```
      ‖A                |
Well, she works in an of‑fice now
        |D               |
And she guesses the pays all right.
        |A               |
She can buy a few new things to wear
   |A                    |E
And still go out at night.
        |A               |
And as soon as she gets home from work
            |D                   |
She wants to be out with the crowd,
              |A                 |
Where she can dance and toss her head   back
   |E              |A            |
And laugh out loud.
```

Verse 4

```
      ‖A                    |
Well, the music's playing fast
   |D              |
And they just met.
   |A                 |
He presses up against   her
              |A                    |E
And his shirt's   all soaked with sweat.
              |A                     |
And with her back against the bar
   |D                  |
She can listen to the band.
      |A              |
And she's holding a Coron‑a
   |E               |A              |
And it's cold against her hand.
```

Repeat Chorus

```
                    |A      |D      |A      |D      |A        ‖
Don't want it to end.
```

My Baby Thinks He's a Train

Written by Leroy Preston

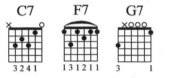

Verse 1

|C7 |
It's three A. M. in the morn - ing.

      |C7 |
The train   whistle is blow - in'.

   |F7 |
It sounds like some lonesome song

          |C7 |
Got in my soul,   in my soul.

   |G7 |F7 |C7 | ||
My baby spent the bank and he won't be back no more.

Verse 2

C7 |
   My baby thinks he's a train.

   |C7 | |
He makes his whistle stop, then he's gone again.

F7 | |C7 | |
   Sometimes it's hard   on a poor girl's brain,   a poor girl's brain.

G7 |F7 |C7 | ||
   I'm telling you, boys,   my baby thinks he's a train.

Bridge

F7 |
Locomotion's the way he moves.

  |**C7** | |
He drags me 'round just like an old caboose.

F7 | | |
  I'm telling you, girls,   that man's insane.

  |**C7**   **G7** |**C7** ||
My baby thinks he's a train.

C7 |
Verse 3
Choo, choo rages on;   the train sound.

       |**C7** |
It's the noise that you hear when my baby hits town.

       |**F7** | |**C7** |
With his long hair flyin',   man, he's hard to take.

  |**G7** |**F7** |**C7** | ||
Oh, what you s'posed to do when   your baby thinks he's a train?

C7 |
Verse 4
  He eats money like a train eats coal.

  |**C7** |
He burns it up   and leaves you in the smoke.

       |**F7** | |**C7** |
If you wanna catch a ride,   you wait till he un - winds.

  |**G7** |**F7** |**C7** | ||
He's just like a train, and he always gives some tramp a ride.

Repeat Bridge

My Maria

Words and Music by
Daniel J. Moore and B.W. Stevenson

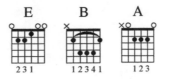

| E | B | A |

Verse 1

My Mari - a,

| E   B   A | |

Don't you know I have come a long, long way?

E   B   A |

I've been longin' to see   her.

| E   B   A |

When she's around   she takes my blues a - way.

| E   B   A |

Sweet Mari - a,

| E   B   A | |

The sunlight   surely hurts my eyes.

E   B   A | | E   B   A |

I'm a lonely dream - er on a high - way in the skies,

Chorus

|| E   B   A | E |A B A E|

Ma - ri   -   a,

| E   B   A | E

Ma - ri,

| A   E | | B A| | E B A|

Ma - ria, I love you.

Verse 2

```
        ‖E       B    A |
My  Mari  -  a,

                   |E        B        A     |              |
There  were  some  blue  and  sorrowed  times.

E          B        A      |                  |
     Just  my  thoughts  a - bout     you  bring  back

E      B        A      |
     My  peace  of  mind.

        |E       B   A |
Gypsy  la - dy,

        |E        B        A   |              |
You're  a  miracle  work  for  me.

E        B      A   |
     You  set  my  soul      free  like  a

    |E       B    A  |              |
Ship     sailin'  on  the  sea.

B                  |A                  |N.C. E      B      A   |              |
     She  is  the  sun  -  light  when  the      skies      are     grey.

B                    A |
     She  treats  me  so      right.

             |N.C. E      B     A  |          |N.C.  E      B    A |
Lady,                take     me  a - way.
```


Repeat Chorus (2X)

Ring of Fire

Words and Music by
Merle Kilgore and June Carter

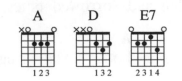

Verse 1

A | D |A |D |A |
Love   is a burning thing

         |A | E7 |A |E7 |A | |
And it makes   a fiery ring.

A | D |A |D |A | |
Bound   by wild de - sires,

A |E7 |A | ||
I fell into a ring of fire.

Chorus

E7 | |D |A
I fell in - to a burning ring of fire.

     |E7 | |D |A
I went down,   down,   down,   and the flames went higher.

     |A | | E7 |A |
And it burns, burns, burns,   the ring of fire,

    E7 |A |
The ring of fire.

Verse 2

```
         ||A          |     D   |A          |D    |A          |
         The  taste       of  love  is  sweet

          |A          |      E7  |A          |E7   |A          |          |
         When  hearts         like  ours  meet.

         A          |D   |A   |      |D    |A   |      |      |
         I  fell  for  you  like  a  child

         A          |      E7     |A          |      ||
         Oh,              but  the  fire  went  wild.
```

Repeat Chorus

Tag

```
            ||A          |          |      E7   |A          |          |
            And it  burns,    burns,    burns,       the  ring  of  fire,

             E7   |A          |      E7   |A          ||
            The  ring  of  fire,         the  ring  of  fire.
```

Round About Way

Words and Music by
Steve Dean and Wil Nance

D   G   C   A

Intro   D | | | |G | |

Verse 1
‖D
As far as all   my friends can tell,
|D | |G |
I took her leaving well.   That's kind-a right,
|D | |
'Cause when I'm out with them,
D | |G |
I don't let her mem - 'ry rule the night.
|C | |D |
For the most part I'm o - kay,
|C | |D | |G |
But I still miss her in a round about   way.

Chorus

```
 ‖D       |       |       |      |G          |
```
A - round a - bout the time that midnight rolls around,
```
          |D      |       |      |      |G          |
```
That's a - round a - bout the time my tears start falling down,
```
                  |A              |
```
'Cause she's not around.
```
          |C              |
```
I come unwound
```
          |A              |
```
And my heart breaks.
```
          |D      |      |   |           |G      |       ‖
```
Yeah, I still miss her in a round about   way.

Interlude

```
D            |            |            |      |G          |
```


Verse 2

```
                  ‖D           |
```
I no long - er sit alone
```
          |D              |           |G          |
```
For hours by the phone   wishing she would call.
```
          |D              |
```
And just the other day
```
          |D              |           |G          |
```
I took her smilin' face   down off my wall.
```
          |C      |           |D      |
```
I've come a long, long way,
```
          |C      |       |D   |           |G      |
```
But I still miss her in a round about   way.

Repeat Chorus

Outro

```
D            |            |            |      |G          ‖
```

Satin Sheets

Words and Music by
John E. Volinkaty

G7	D	G	A7

Intro |N.C.(G7) | |D | | |

Chorus

D | |G | |
Satin sheets to lie on,   satin pillows to cry on,

D | |A7 | |
Still, I'm not happy don't you see?

D | |G | |
Big long Cadillac,   tailor-mades u - pon my back,

D |A7 |D | |
Still, I want you to set me free.

Verse

D | |G |
I've found an - other man   who can give more than you can,

|D | |A7 | |
Though you've given me ev'ry - thing money can buy.

D | |G | |
But your money can't hold me tight like he does on a long, long night.

D |A7 |D | |
You know you didn't keep me satis - fied.

Repeat Chorus

Repeat Chorus

Repeat Chorus & fade

Small Town Saturday Night

Words and Music by
Pat Alger and Hank DeVito

C   G   D   Em

Intro

```
C   G    |D   G    |C   G    |D            |

G        |         |         |             |
```

Verse 1

```
        ‖G                |D   |G       |         |
There's an Elvis movie on the marquee sign
C    G        |D   |G       |         |
We've all seen at least  three times.
G            |D         |G       |
Everybody's broke, Bobby's got a buck.
    |C          G       |D   |G       |
Put a dollar's worth of gas in his pickup truck.
```

Chorus 1

```
        ‖C                           |
We're going ninty miles an hour down a dead end road.
    |G                   |D      |Em      |
What's  the hurry, son; where  you gonna go?
            |C         G   |D            G
We're gonna  howl at the moon,   shoot out the light.
    |C     G   |D         G
It's a   small town Saturday night.
    |C     G   |D         |G       |         |
It's a   small town Saturday night.
C   G    |D   |G       |
```

Verse 2

```
        ‖G                        |D      |G          |
Lucy's  got her lipstick on a little too bright.
     |C          G          |D        |G          |
Bob - by's getting drunk and look - ing for a fight.
     |G                         |D      |G          |
Liq - uor on his breath and trou - ble on his mind.
     |C       G    |D     |G         |
And Lucy's just a kid along   for the ride.
```

Chorus 2

```
        ‖C                       |
Got a six-pack of beer and a bottle of wine.
     |G              |D       |Em        |
Got - ta be bad just to have a good time.
                |C       G    |D           G
They're gonna   howl at the moon,   shoot out the light.
     |C    G  |D          G
It's a   small town Saturday night.
     |C    G  |D          |G         |          |
It's a   small town Saturday night.
C    G     |D    G    |C    G    |D          |G          |
```

Verse 3

```
        ‖G                       |D    |G       |          |
Bob - by told Lucy, "The world  ain't round;
C    G         |D    |G       |
Drops off sharp at the edge of town.
     |G                   |D      |G          |
Lu - cy, you know the world   must be flat
            |C       G    |D     |G       |
'Cause when people leave town, they never come back."
```

80

Chorus 3

```
                  ‖C                                    |
          They go ninety miles an hour to the city limits sign,
                 |G                        |D         |Em          |
          Put the pedal to the metal 'fore they change their mind.
               |C         G   |D             G
          They   howl at the moon,    shoot out the light.

               |C       G  |D            G
          It's a    small town Saturday night.

               |C         G  |D              |Em         |
          Yeah,    howl at the moon,    shoot out the light.

                   |C       G  |D             G
          Yeah, it's a    small town Saturday night.

               |C       G  |D            G
          It's a    small town Saturday night.

               |C       G  |D            |G         |              |
          It's a    small town Saturday night.

          C       G      |D    G      ‖
```

Shut Up and Kiss Me

Words and Music by
Mary Chapin Carpenter

D   C   G   A

Intro

D   C |G |D   C |G |

D   C |G |D   C |G ||

Verse 1

D   C |G |
Don't mean to get a little forward with you.
D   C |G |
Don't mean to get ahead of where we are.
D   C |G |
Don't mean to act a little nervous around you;
D   C |G
Just a little nervous about   my heart.

Chorus 1

||C   D |G |
'Cause it's been a - while since I felt this feeling
C   D |G |
That every - thing that you do gives me.
C   D |G |C   D |
It's been too long since somebody whispered,   ooh,
G |D   C |G |D   C |G ||
"Shut up and kiss me."

Verse 2

```
        D           C        |G          |
        Didn't ex - pect to be in this position.
        D           C        |G            |
        Didn't ex - pect to have to rise above
        D           C     |G         |
        My repu - tation for cynicism;
        D           C          |G
        Been a jaded lady when it comes to love.
```

Chorus 2

```
        ||C    D        |G                |
        But  oh, baby, just to feel this feeling
        C           D     |G               |
        That every - thing that you do gives me.
        C            D       |G              |C    D     |
        It's been too long since somebody whispered,    ooh,
        G                    ||
        "Shut up and kiss me."
```

Bridge

```
        A                        |         |
        There's something 'bout the silent type
        C         D      |G        |
        Attracting me to you.
        A                |          |
        All business, baby, none of the hype
        C                |         ||
        That no talker can live up to.
```

Interlude

```
        D    C    |G          |D    C    |G          |

        D    C    |G          |D    C    |G          |

        D    C    |G          |D    C    |G          |

        D    C    |G          |D    C    |G          ||
```

Verse 3

```
D        C          |G                |
Come closer, baby; I can't hear you.
D          C          |G               |
Just an - other whisper, if you please.
D        C           |G
Don't worry 'bout the details, darling.
    |D            C          |G          ||
You've got the kind of mind I love  to read.
```

Verse 4

```
D        C            |G                  |
Talk is cheap and, baby, time's expensive.
D          C          |G               |
So why waste another minute more?
D            C         |G
And life's too short to be so apprehensive.
    |D            C             |G          ||
Love's  as much the symptom, darling, as the cure.
```

Chorus 3

```
C    D          |G                  |
Oh baby, when I feel this feeling,
C        D      |G                |
It's like genuine voodoo hits me.
C          D        |G                   |C    D   |G      ||
It's been too long since somebody whispered,   ooh...
```

Chorus 4

```
C     D       |G                |
    Oh  baby,  I  can  feel  this  feeling
C         D        |G                |
    That  every - thing  that  you  do  gives  me.
C           D        |G                    |C      D      |
    It's  been  too  long  since  somebody  whispered,    ooh,
G                      |C     D  |G            |
"Shut  up  and  kiss  me."    Ooh,  ooh.
C    D  |G                    |C     D  |G          ||
    Ooh.      "Shut  up  and  kiss  me."
```

Thank God I'm a Country Boy

Words and Music by
John Martin Sommers

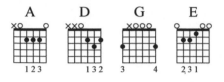

Verse 1

     |**A** | **D**
Well, life on a farm is kinda laid back.

     |**A** |**G**   **D**
Ain't much an old country boy like me can't hack.

     |**A** | **D**
It's early to rise,   early in the sack.

        |**A**   **E** |**A**
Thank God I'm a country boy.

     |**A** | **D** |
A simple kinda life never did me no harm,

A |**G**   **D**
Raisin' me a family and workin' on a farm.

     |**A** | **D**
My days are all filled with an easy country charm.

     |**A**   **E** |**A**
Thank God I'm a country boy.

Chorus

        ||**E** |**A**
Well, I got me a fine wife, I got me old fiddle.

       |**E** |**A**
When the sun's comin' up I got cakes on the griddle.

     |**A** | **D**
And life ain't nothin' but a funny, funny, riddle.

     |**A**   **E** |**A**
Thank God I'm a country boy.

Verse 2

      ‖**A** | **D**
When the work's all done and the sun's settin' low,

  |**A** |**G**   **D**
I pull out my fiddle and I rosin up the bow.

    |**A** | **D**
But the kids are asleep so I keep it kinda low.

    |**A**   **E** |**A**
Thank God I'm a country boy.

  |**A** | **D**
I'd play "Sally Goodin'" all   day if I could,

   |**A** |**G**   **D**
But the Lord and my wife wouldn't take it very good.

   |**A** | **D**
So I fiddle when I can and I work when I should.

   |**A**   **E** |**A**
Thank God I'm a country boy.

Repeat Chorus

Verse 3

     ‖**A** | **D**
Well, I wouldn't trade my life for diamonds or jewels.

 |**A** |**G**   **D**
I never was one of them money - hungry fools.

  |**A** | **D**
I'd rather have my fiddle and my farmin' tools.

   |**A**   **E** |**A**
Thank God I'm a country boy.

   |**A** | **D**
Yeah, city folk drivin' in a black limou - sine;

 |**A** |**G**   **D**
A lotta sad people thinkin' that's mighty keen.

    |**A** | **D**
Well, folks, let me tell you now ex - actly what I mean:

   |**A**   **E** |**A**
I thank God I'm a country boy.

Verse 4

       ||A | D
Well, my fiddle was my daddy's till the day he died,

     |A |G   D
And he took me by the hand and held me close to his side.

      |A | D
He said, "Live a good life and play my fiddle with pride

      |A   E |A
And thank God you're a country boy."

    |A | D
My daddy taught me young how to hunt and how too whittle.

    |A |G   D
He taught me how to work and play a tune on the fiddle.

    |A | D
He taught me how to love and how to give just a little.

     |A   E |A
Thank God I'm a country boy.

Repeat Chorus

When You Say Nothing at All

Words and Music by
Don Schlitz and Paul Overstreet

D   A   G

Intro | D   A | G   A | D   A | G   A ||

Verse 1

   D   A
It's amaz - ing how you

G   A | D   A | G   A |
Can speak right   to my heart.

D   A
Without say - ing a word

G   A | D   A | G   A |
You can light up the dark.

G | A
Try as I may, I could nev - er explain

D   A | G | A |
What I hear   when you don't   say a thing.

Chorus 1

```
        ‖D                A          |G              A
The smile on your face  lets me know  that you need  me.
                 |D                 A           |G              A
There's a truth in your eyes  saying you'll  never leave  me.
              |D                  A
The touch of your hand
                              |G           |A         |G      A     |
Says you'll catch  me if ever I fall.
G              |A                              |D      A    |G      A        |
You say it best    when you say nothing at all.
D        A      |G        A       ‖
```

Verse 2

```
        D              A             |
   All day long   I can hear
G            A            |D    A   |G    A        |
   People talk - ing out loud,
D              A               |
   But when you   hold me near
G      A                    |D      A    |G    A        |
    You drown out the crowd.
G                         |A            |
Old Mister Webster could nev - er define
D              A          |G         |A
What's being said  between your   heart and mine.
```

Repeat Chorus 1

```
        D    A   |G           |A           |G
```

90

Chorus 2

   ‖D   A |G   A
The smile on your face lets me know that you need me.

        |D   A   G | |
There's a truth in your eyes saying you'll never leave me.

   |D   A
The touch of your hand

          |G |A |G   A |
Says you'll catch me if ever I fall.

G |A |D A |G |
You say it best when you say nothing at all.

D   A |G   A |D   ‖

This One's for the Girls

Words and Music by
Aimee Mayo, Hillary Lindsey and Chris Lindsey

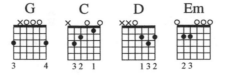

Verse 1

G |C |D | |
This is for all you girls about thirteen.

G |C |D |
High school can be so rough, can be so mean.

|Em |C |D |
Hold on to,   on   to your innocence.

D |Em |C |D
Stand your ground   when ev - 'rybody's givin' in.

|D ||
This one's for the girls.

Verse 2

G |C |D | |
This is for all you girls about twenty - five

G |C |D |
In little apart - ments,   just try - ing to get by,

|Em |C |D |
Livin' on,   on dreams   and Spaghetti - O's,

D |Em |C |D
Wond'rin' where   your life is gonna go.

Chorus

|D ||G
This   one's for the girls   who've ev - er had a broken heart,

C   Em | D
Who've wished   upon a shooting star.

G | |C
You're beau - tiful the way you are.

D | |G
This one's for the girls   who love   without holdin' back,

C   Em | D |C |D
Who dream with ev - 'rything they have,   all around   the world.

|D |G |C |D | ||
This   one's for the girls.   (This one's for   all the girls.)

Verse 3

G |C |D
This is for all   you girls about forty - two

G |C |D
Tossin' pen - nies into the foun - tain of youth.

|Em |C |D
Ev'ry laugh,   laugh line   on your face

D |Em |C |D
Made you who   you are   today.

Repeat Chorus

Bridge

C |G |D | |
Yeah,   we're all the same   inside. (The same   inside.)

C |G |D
From one   to ninety - nine.

Repeat Chorus

Outro

|D |G |C |
Yeah, this one's for the girls. (This one's for   all the girls.)

D   Em | D   G | ||

Two Piña Coladas

Words and Music by
Sandy Mason, Benita Marie Hill
and Shawn Camp

D   A   G

Intro   D | | |

Verse 1

‖D |
I was feeling the blues, I was watching the news
   |D |A
When this fella came on the T - V.
   |A |
He said, "I'm telling you that science has proven
   |A |D |
That heartaches are healed by the sea."
G |
That got me going with - out even knowing;
|D |G
I packed right up and drove down.
   |G |D
Now I'm on a roll and I swear   on my soul
   |D   A |D
To - night I'm gonna paint this town.

Chorus 1

```
      |A        ‖D              |
So bring me two piña cola - das;
        |D                |A
I want one for each hand.
      A      |A               |
Let's set sail  with Captain Mor - gan,
          |A                |D
Oh, and never leave dry land.
  |G              |
Hey, troubles, I forgot  'em;
 |D                     |G
I buried 'em in the sand.
           |G          |D
So bring me two piña cola - das;
            |D      A       |D       |
She said good - bye to her good-timing man.
G            |D          |    A    |D           |
```

Verse 2

```
        ‖D                  |
Oh, now I've gotta say that the wind and the waves
        |D                |A        |
And the moon winking down at me
A                  |
Eases my mind by leaving behind
   |A                     |D
The heartaches that love often  brings.
   |G               |
Now I've got a smile that goes on for miles
   |D             |G
With no inclination to roam.
   |G                     |D
And I've gotta say that I think   I've gotta stay
           |D           A      |D
'Cause this is feeling more and more like home.
```

Repeat Chorus (2x)

Wide Open Spaces

Words and Music by
Susan Gibson

D   Em7   G   A

Verse 1

D   Em7 |D
Who doesn't know what I'm talking about?

D   Em7 |D
Who's never left home, who's never struck out

       |G   D |
To find a dream and a life of their own,

       |G | A ||
A place   in the clouds, a founda-tion of stone?

Verse 2

D   Em7 |D |
Many pre-cede and many will follow,

D   Em7 |D
A young girl's dreams no longer hollow.

       |G   D |
It takes the shape of a place out west.

       |G | A
But what it holds   for her she hasn't yet guessed.

Chorus

       ||D   Em7 |G   A |
She needs   wide open spac - es,

D   Em7 |G   A
Room to make   her big mis - takes.

       |D   Em7 |G
She needs   new   fac-es.

    A |D   Em7 |G   A ||
She knows the high stakes.

Verse 3
   D   Em7 |D |
   She traveled this road as a child,

   D   Em7 |D
   Wide-eyed and grinning, she never tired.

              |G   D |
   But now she won't be coming back with the rest.

              |G | A
   If these are life's   lessons, she'll take this test.

Repeat Chorus

Bridge
   D   G |D |
   As her folks drive a-way, her dad yells, "Check the oil."

                   G |D
   Mom stares out the window and says, "I'm leavin' my girl."

           |G   D |
   She said, "It didn't seem like that long a-go"

           |G | A ||
   When she stood   there and let her own folks know she needed…

Outro-Chorus
   D   Em7 |G   A |
   Wide open spac-es,

   D   Em7 |G   A
   Room to make   her big mis-takes.

          |D   Em7 |G
   She needs new   fac-es.

    A |D
   She knows the high stakes.

    Em7 |G   A |D
   She knows the high stakes, she knows the high stakes.

    Em7 |G   A |D   Em7 |G
   Wide open spac-es, she knows the high stakes.

    A |D   Em7 |G   A |D Em7 |G A D ||
   She knows the high stakes, wide open spac-es.

You're Easy on the Eyes

Words and Music by
Terri Clark, Chris Waters
and Tom Shapiro

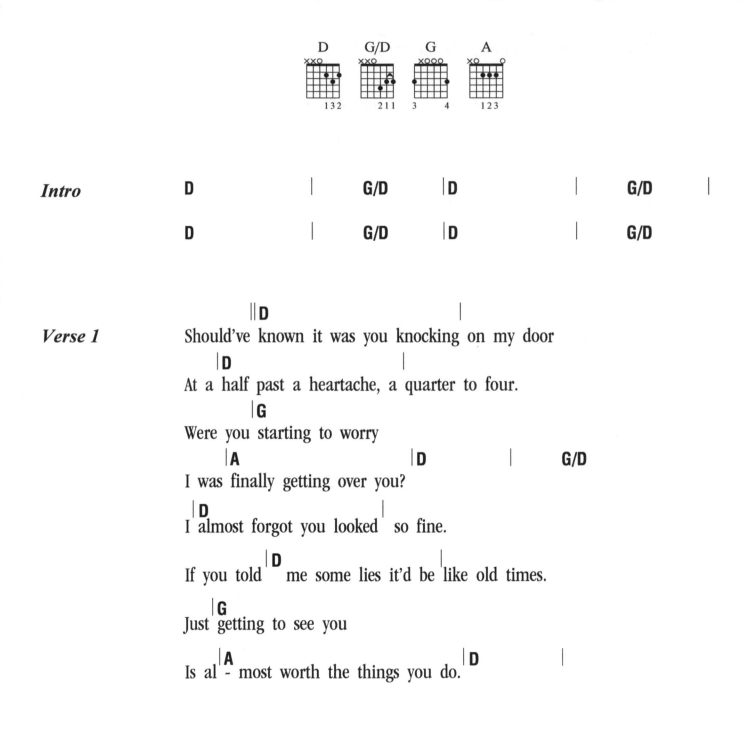

Intro

| D | | G/D | D | | G/D | |

| D | | G/D | D | | G/D |

Verse 1

‖ D |
Should've known it was you knocking on my door

| D |
At a half past a heartache, a quarter to four.

| G
Were you starting to worry

| A | D | G/D
I was finally getting over you?

| D |
I almost forgot you looked so fine.

| D |
If you told me some lies it'd be like old times.

| G
Just getting to see you

| A | D |
Is al - most worth the things you do.

Chorus

```
                    ‖D              |
You're easy on the eyes,
                  |D              |
Hard on the heart.
               |A                       |
You look so good, but the way things look
              G        |D           |
Ain't the way they are.
                 |G            |
Better say good - bye
                       |A             |
Before this goes too far
                 |G                   |A
'Cause now I real - ize you're easy on the eyes,
                     |D        | G/D   |D         | G/D
Hard on the heart.
```

Verse 2

```
          ‖D                  |
I've got to admit you  got a smile
    |D                  |
That really reeled me in  for a while,
    |G
But it ain't funny,
    |A                           |D          | G/D
Hon - ey, what you put me through.
    |D                        |
So, why don't you send me your  photograph?
    |D                |
It'd hurt a lot less than tak - ing you back.
    |G
Then I could still have
        |A                  |D           |
My fa - vorite part of you.
```

Repeat Chorus (2x)

You're Still the One

Words and Music by
Shania Twain and R.J. Lange

D   G   A   Em

Intro

N.C. |D |
When I first saw you,   I saw love.

G |D |
And the first time you touched me,   I felt love.

G |
And after all this time,

D |G   A ||
You're still the one I love.

Verse 1

D |
Looks like we made it.

G   A |
Look how far we've come,   my baby.

D |
We might-a took the long way.

G   A ||
We knew we'd get   there someday.

Pre-Chorus

D |G   A
They said, "I bet   they'll never make   it."

      |D   G |A
But just look at us holding on.

            |D   G |A   G
We're still togeth - er, still going strong.

Chorus 1

```
                          ‖ D                              G      |
(You're still the one.)    You're still the one I run  to,
   Em                           A       |
   The one that I belong   to.
   D                              G  |A     G
   You're still the one I want   for life.
                          |D                              G       |
(You're still the one.)    You're still the one that I  love,
   Em                           A       |
   The only one I dream   of.
   D                              G     |A          ‖
   You're still the one I kiss   good - night.
```

Verse 2

```
   D                          |
   Ain't nothin' better;
   G                  A           |
   We beat the odds   together.
   D                             |
   I'm glad we didn't lisen.
   G                  A              ‖
   Look  at what we would   be missing.
```

Repeat Pre-Chorus

Chorus 2

        ‖**D**   **G** |
(You're still the one.)   You're still the one I run to,

Em   **A** |
   The one that I belong to.

D   **G** |**A**   **G**
  You're still the one I want for life.

                       |**D**   **G** |
(You're still the one.)   You're still the one that I love,

Em   **A** |
   The only one I dream of.

D   **G** |**A** |
   You're still the one I kiss good - night. You're still the one.

D   **G** |**A** |**D**   **G** |**A**

Repeat Chorus 1

Outro

        D |
   I'm so glad we made it.

G   **A** | ‖
Look how far we've come, my baby.